HOME

© C. Baxter Kruger, Ph.D. 2023

Home
ISBN: 979-8-9851553-2-7
Written by C. Baxter Kruger
© C. Baxter Kruger Ph.D. 2023
First published 1994, republished 2023

About the Author

Baxter has been married to Beth for 40 years. They have four children and four grandchildren and live in Brandon, Mississippi. He received his Ph.D. at Kings College, Aberdeen University in Scotland under Professor James. B. Torrance. Dr. Kruger is the author of 9 books, including the international bestsellers, *The Shack Revisited, Patmos*, and his early small book, *The Parable of the Dancing God*, numerous essays, and hundreds of hours of teaching, and a variety of online studies—all available at perichoresis.org. Dr. Kruger has traveled the world for 30 years proclaiming the good news of our inclusion in Jesus and his relationship with his Father in the Spirit. He enjoys cooking crawfish, hand carving fishing lures, playing golf, and loves spending time with his grandchildren.

Foreword: Professor Trevor Hart
Cover Design: Tom Carroll, South Australia
Layout: Karen Thompson, Western Australia

To my daughter
CAROLINE WILLIAMS KRUGER

and my Grandparents
JAMES E. BAXTER
THELMA F. BAXTER

who now know as they are known

Other Titles Available From
C. Baxter Kruger:

A Note on the Word *Perichoresis*

Genuine acceptance removes fear and hiding, and creates freedom to know and be known. In this freedom arises a fellowship and sharing so honest and open and real that the persons involved dwell in one another. There is union without loss of individual identity. When one weeps, the other tastes salt. It is only in the Triune relationship of Father, Son and Spirit that personal relationship of this order exists, and the early Church used the word "perichoresis" to describe it. The good news is that Jesus Christ has drawn us within this relationship and its fullness and life are to be played out in each of us and in all creation.

For more information on Baxter Kruger or Perichoresis visit Perichorises.org

Contents

Foreword

Home, so the purveyors of popular lore and peddlers of sentimental schmaltz would have us believe, is where the heart is. This is a popular but ultimately self-deluding picture which resonates with the individualistic and self-serving ethos of western culture, and serves conveniently to justify our determination to choose for ourselves just where and with whom we shall be, shaping our own identities. Baxter Kruger offers a different account of the matter for our consideration in this book. Home, he suggests, is where we belong, and that may well be somewhere quite different from the present temporary focus of our longings, desires and hankerings. In practice it often is, which is part of the reason for the deep-down sense of alienation and cosmic loneliness which so many people feel in life. Attaching ourselves emotionally now to this and then to that surrogate host, distracting ourselves with every form of narcotic experience, we crave ever deeper satisfaction, and fail to recognise our restless and insatiat condition for what it is—a form of existential homesickness.

Where, then, is home? What is the source of the "inconsolable dream" which plagues us in the midst of our dislocation and lostness? Dr. Kruger leaves us in no doubt about its identity. Home is not so much a place, but a set of relationships within which we properly belong (and indeed within which we actually exist whether our lifestyle acknowledges and reflects the fact or not)—namely our identity as sons and daughters of a Heavenly Father, brothers and sisters of an eternal Son who has made our lot his own in order to share his Father's love with us in our orphaned state, and recipients of a Spirit who grants us the faith to embrace our filial inheritance with both hands and rejoice in it. This is where we truly belong, and until it is also where our heart is, we shall continue to be restless and dissatisfied, living a lie and unable to quench the existential thirst which it creates.

This, then, is a book about the gospel. But it is a book written just as much for those within the church as for those outside it. For the sorry truth of the matter is that the vast majority of Christian men and women, for whatever reason, have not yet properly laid hold of the truth contained in the powerful metaphor around which this book is woven. We do not, in our hearts rather than our heads anyway, perceive ourselves as really belonging to God. Too often the God who is preached from our pulpits, and who inhabits our Christian imagination, is a God who at root is against us rather than for us, who is waiting for an opportunity to condemn or to cast us off, rather than to embrace and restore and heal us.

The parable which Jesus told about the wayward son who took his inheritance early and left home can be read in many different ways. Viewed from one angle the story of the son's approach to his "home" can be seen as a parable of Christian religiosity. We think that where we really belong is with the pigs in the far country, and we approach God with the intention merely of receiving a place as a hired servant in his household. Somehow, even though we know the glorious facts of the gospel—that the fatted calf has been slaughtered, that the ring has been placed on our finger and new shoes on our feet, that a banquet has been arranged in our honour—we can't quite connect with all this in our heart. We can't, perhaps dare not, believe that the one whom the Father rushes out to meet when still far off, fathoming the very depths of hell itself, and bears home rejoicing, is actually us. Surely there must be some mistake? Surely it must be someone else?

Like King David we need to hear the prophetic declaration, "You are the one." This parable is about you and not someone else. We still have to come to terms with the fact that this is what our God is like, that here (and not in the pigsty) is where we belong, and that nothing we have done or can do will ever change that. What God has done for us in Jesus Christ cannot now be undone. If we are not clear on this then we labour under the burden of some inadequate and frankly sub Christian picture of God—a God quite different from the one revealed in Jesus Christ—and it is an overwhelming burden, far too heavy for us to bear.

This book seeks to share in the liberating of Christians from that false burden. It addresses themes and doctrines at the very heart of Christian theology—trinity, incarnation, atonement and so on. Yet it does so in a way which wonderfully connects these themes with the real world of Christian life under God, rather than the dry and dusty environment of the textbook. And it does so in a way which shows how they are a vital component of the gospel itself. The style is clear and lively, and filled with illustrations and examples which root the argument firmly in the mesh of our shared existence as human beings. My hope is that it may be used to enable many, both within the church and without, to find the way home.

Professor Trevor Hart
St. Mary's College
University of St. Andrews

CHAPTER 1

The Inconsolable Dream[1]

Home is among the most evocative and haunting words in our language. Like any other word, it is simply an arrangement of consonants and vowels, yet it possesses the uncanny capacity to speak volumes to us and an almost magical ability to touch our souls. Why is this? What is it about this word? Why does it seem to have such a special ability to touch us so deeply?

If we search the dictionaries for a definition, we find that one of the most common usages of *home* is as a synonym for "habitation" or "house." Home is the place where one lives or dwells, our fixed residence. Home also functions as a synonym of "origin." America is the home of baseball. Paris is the home of fashion. In sports, home is often used to refer to the goal or end of the game. To make it home, for example, is the goal of baseball. In golf, the last nine holes are called the homeward half and the eighteenth green is often affectionately thought of as home.

While these are all common, and technically correct, usages

---

1 The phrase "the inconsolable dream" owes much to C. S. Lewis' phrase "the inconsolable secret" found in his stimulating essay, "The Weight of Glory." See his book, *The Weight of Glory and Other Addresses* (Grand Rapids: Wm. B. Eerdmans Pub. Co., sixth printing, 1975), p. 4.

of the word, everyone knows that they are peripheral to another meaning. Beyond home as the place of residence or the origin of something or the goal toward which something moves, there remains a more profound meaning which is woven into the fabric of something very deep within us and dear to us. And it is this deeper meaning that accounts for the special power of the word.

Of course, the million dollar question is what is this deeper meaning? And why is it deeper? Why is it so dear to us? Herein lies the difficulty, for it answers to these types of questions that prove to be so frustratingly elusive. They seem so impossible to grasp and reduce to clear thought. But we do have some leads in the right direction. The best one, to me, is the way we sometimes use home as a synonym for being in one's element: "Holley is so at home with cooking."

When we speak of someone being in her element, we mean far more than that she is simply in the right place. We mean she is where she belongs. We mean she is in her niche, in an environment which is quite natural to her, custom-made for her, so much so that there is not the slightest hint of foreignness or alienation. There is no head wind, so to speak, no interference or red tape, no against-the-grain lie as sometimes happens to a good shot in golf. Everything is right, suitable, perfectly matched.

Like the idea of "peace," which means both the absence of conflict and the presence of wholeness, "being in our element" means both the absence of frustration and stifling and the presence of flourishing and thriving. Everything is in harmony, in sync, and like children at play, spontaneous, free-flowing, utterly lost to the dis-ease of selfconsciousness.

Taking note of the connection between "home" and "being in

our element" helps us to see that the deeper meaning of home has to do with being where we belong, where things are right for us. Moreover, it helps us to understand that home has to do with the spontaneity, flourishing and thriving of that belonging. Home is where things are so well-suited to us that we are not only at peace, but thrive and are set free to fire on all cylinders. But now a further question arises: What is the "belonging" that we are speaking of here, the belonging that generates human flourishing? What is the "element" that produces such spontaneity and thriving joy?

It is quite correct to say that books belong on a bookshelf and that a golf ball belongs with golf clubs, but obviously this kind of belonging leaves us well short of the kind that generates human flourishing. Something happens to the nuance of the word "belonging" when we take it out of the context of books and bookshelves and move it into the human context. A new level of meaning is introduced. The idea becomes personal and relational. With books and bookshelves, belonging has to do with tradition and custom—a bookshelf is where books have always been placed. It also has to do with design and inanimate physical congruency—the bookshelves are designed to accommodate books.

We could, of course, quite rightly use "belonging" in this way of human beings—we belong on earth, in an environment of sunlight, air and water. The earth and human life are designed for each other, physically right. Nevertheless, there remains another level of meaning when we speak of the "belonging" of human beings, especially when we are talking about it in the context of flourishing and thriving.

Doesn't the key lie in the way the ideas of flourishing and

thriving somehow nudge us to translate "belonging" into personal relationship? Isn't "being in our element" not merely flourishing and thriving of any sort, but the particular flourishing and thriving of right relationship with another person? And is this not what the word *home* really means to us, to *belong* to another *person*, to *flourish* and *thrive* in that belonging?

But then there is another question—what does it mean to belong to another person? Are we talking about friendship, the event of courtship or the institution of marriage? Obviously belonging involves a relationship to some degree. But even here it is not simply a matter of relationship *per se*. For relationships could easily be merely tolerable as when Mabel "just grins and bears" Fred. Or they could be outwardly adorned, politically correct and by-the-book, but empty.

The human belonging that produces flourishing and thriving in us has to do with a relationship of *personal hospitality*. Both words need to be emphasized. "Hospitality" carries us into the arena of being welcomed. We are not ignored nor looked past, not turned away nor abandoned, but personally noticed. Our presence is acknowledged and we are called by name. And in the calling of our name we are not simply endured, but welcomed; not neglected, but received, accepted and embraced. And "personal" makes sure that we realize that what is so accepted and received is not a piece of firewood or a bit of information or an outward image, but a person. *We* are not ignored, but welcomed.

Many a child knows that awful dread that flashes through her being when she is solemnly called by her full name. The feeling of pure trouble short-circuits every spark of freedom and kicks the transmission into the overdrive of atoning, hoop-jumping,

I'll-do- anything performance. There is, needless to say, a radical cessation of freedom to be herself.

The "belonging" of which we are speaking here moves us in the opposite direction. The calling of belonging invites us, summons us—indeed, commands and actually liberates us—to unveil ourselves and be known. There is something in the call that frees us from fear and shame, that takes away our reservation and guardedness, that slays the temptation to use masks or camouflage. For we are called—not a dressed up form of ourselves or the projection of an acceptable image, but the real us. *We* are touched, summoned and called forth.

Surely a key component in being so called is acceptance. It is acceptance that triggers the liberty to show ourselves, relax all pretense and simply be who we are. The belonging of human beings which gives birth to flourishing has to do with being called in such acceptance. But there is more to belonging than acceptance, critical as it is. Acceptance is still too neutral. More needs to be said. The pride in our father's eye, the calming warmth and safety of our mother's touch, and the liberating call of our name surely express being noticed and accepted and embraced, but they express so much more, don't they? They express being appreciated and valued. They express being *cherished*.

Now we are moving to the heart of the matter. For to be cherished means to be the object of pure delight—the apple of someone's eye. It means to be prized, treasured. Without the idea of being cherished, "belonging" is too much like caffeine free diet Coke—adequate, but short on body, depth and flavor. But "cherished," this is the intangible that fills "belonging" with "*flourishing*" and "*thriving joy*." For it tells us that behind being noticed and behind being called by name and accepted, lies undiluted affection.

Some years back there was an interview on TV with a famous basketball coach. In the course of the interview the discussion shifted from the coach's success on the court to his relationship with his son, who was physically handicapped. As the coach expressed his affection for his son, the interviewer gave it a patronizing, you-feel sorry-for-him, twist. This happened several times and the coach was increasingly perturbed. He finally said, "Look! I not only love my son, I *like* him."

Isn't this the point? When the ideas of "element" and "belonging" are used of human beings, they not only become relational words, they become heart words. In the context of persons, "belonging" speaks of something beyond the absence of conflict, beyond toleration, beyond being noticed, accepted and known. It speaks of the inner circle of someone's devotion and adoration. And more than this, it speaks of being in that circle, of being wanted, desired and longed for. "Belonging" is trying to tell us about being noticed through eyes of affection and delight, about being called by name by someone who takes the greatest pleasure in us. It is trying to tell us about being adored and loved—cherished.

Now, what happens to us when we encounter such affection? Does it deflate us? Does it make us lonely, sad? Does it make us feel lost, empty, hopeless? No, it quickens us. An encounter with such affection thrills and liberates us. It creates a womb of safety, security and hope in which we flourish and soar.

Now, isn't this thrill and liberation, this flourishing and soaring the deepest and most elusive meaning of *home* for us?

Home is not a mere place or static state. It is an event of being. Home is what happens in us and to us as we are summoned by the delighted attention of another person. The summoning quickens the real us, digs at the root of our fearful hiding, cuts through the definitions which translate us into performers, and calls us forth to be. The summoning triggers an event of authenticity, of freedom to be ourselves, to express and give ourselves. The summoning generates an event of reality, of being simply who we are.

But we would miss the forest for the trees if we stopped here. For home is not one-directional, is it? Home involves a second movement besides that of being noticed, called and cherished and the freedom to be which these dynamics trigger. It also involves our noticing and desiring another, our calling them by name and our accepting and cherishing them in return. And thus home is about the reality that comes into being in such a meeting, the life fired in the mix of such mutual acceptance and delight.

Home is what happens when we are noticed and notice, when we are accepted and accept, cherished and cherish. Home is the mysterious reality called into being when *we* are summoned by the delighted acceptance of another person and *they* are summoned by ours. And the mutual summoning converges into a spontaneous, flourishing and thriving fellowship. Isn't home, in its deepest sense, the concert of such a meeting, the *dance of life* birthed in the convergence of such mutual summoning?

Who doesn't want to experience home? Isn't this the longing of our hearts? One suspects that we may have stumbled onto the secret of the word's almost magical ability to speak and conjure. It is not really magic at all, is it? There is no power in the word itself. It cannot reach into our hearts. It cannot bring anything to us or touch us, or say anything to us, for that matter. What it can do is make us aware of something that is already alive within us.

Doesn't the apparent magic of the word lie in the way it reminds us of those moments when *we tasted* the flourishing, thriving joy of such belonging? Doesn't its marvelous capacity to speak volumes to us really come from the fact that it replays the times *we knew* that security, that safety, that affection, that adoration, or when they flowed through us to another, or when we danced in their fellowship?

Isn't *home's* peculiar power to touch us really caused by the way it brings us to feel the pain of knowing that we have only *heard rumors* of such a relationship—that there have only been *moments* when we danced?

Doesn't its capacity to haunt us lie in the fact that it is the particular collection of letters that triggers the memory of *our inconsolable dream* to be baptized in such a belonging and thus lets loose the deeper fear that our dream will never be fulfilled, that it is indeed inconsolable, that we will be left out and miss the dance?

CHAPTER 2

The Mystery

Have we really answered our question about the power of the word home? To a degree, yes. But more must be said. To begin with, more must be asked. Why do we have such a longing within us? Why do we afflict ourselves with such a dream? Why don't we just get on with life like the animals? Why doesn't just being here, just being alive, satisfy us, thrill and fill us?

Isn't there something else here to be said about the haunt of the word? It is not only that the word triggers the memory of our inconsolable dream to belong; it also, and perhaps more importantly, triggers the *faith* in the secret places of our hearts that it is not a dream at all, but our *destiny*.

Isn't this the truth? Don't we *believe* that we are *supposed* to have this kind of relationship? Don't we *believe* that this *is* our element, *our* element? Don't we believe in such a baptism? But why? Who told us such a thing? How have we come to this conclusion? Where would we get such a belief?

The inconsolable dream is not of our own doing. It does not have its origin in us. The dream is the echo of the eternal word of

God which is speaking to us in Jesus Christ. Our longing is the fruit of the Spirit's witness whispering our adoption, proclaiming to us that there is indeed such a relationship and that we have been included in it. Our dream to belong to another, to dwell in that belonging, our belief that we are destined for the concert, and the haunting fear of missing out, arises from the fact that it is no dream at all but the truth.

There is an intriguing verse in the Gospel of John—chapter 14, verse 20—in which Jesus says: "In that day you shall know that I am in My Father, and you in Me, and I in you." The "day" of which Jesus speaks is the day of the Spirit. Jesus is saying that after his work is finished, the Spirit will be given to bear witness to us concerning what he has accomplished. "In that day *you* shall *know*." Here is the origin of our deep longing. In the first instance, it is the result of what Jesus Christ has made of us. In the second instance, it is the result of the fact that we are being addressed in the Spirit. Jesus Christ is our home and he is speaking to us in the Spirit to make sure we know it. In order to gain greater clarity on this, we have to take the time to think through the other parts of this statement.

Jesus' statement breaks down into three phrases: "I am in my Father," "you in me," and "I in you." The central point is Jesus' remarkable relationship with his Father. To this he adds the astounding fact that we are included in it (you in me). And then he says that his relationship with his Father is at work in us now, seeking to be formed in us (I in you).

"I am in my Father." It is odd, is it not, to speak of being "in" another person? Our normal expression of togetherness is to use the word "with." "John is *with* Laura." Jesus, however, does not say that he is "with" his Father; he says he is "in" his Father. This is specialized language. It is designed to make us stop and ponder the nature of Jesus' relationship with his Father. The little preposition "in" is telling us that something quite exceptional and wonderful is going on between the Father and Jesus.

The Christian church has always believed that God is not, strictly speaking, alone. There is one God to be sure, but this one God exists in relationship, in a relationship of three persons. Many have pulled their hair out trying to understand how *three* can possibly equal one. If you take three books and put them together, they remain three books no matter how hard you press them together! You can stack them on top of each other and place a ten ton stone on them, but they will remain three books.

But what if the books managed to read each other? And what if they managed to read each other so thoroughly and perfectly that they all began to say the same thing in their own way? This is something of what the church has come to see about God. There are three distinct persons—Father, Son and Spirit—but they are not separate. They do not live in isolation. They do not hide from one another or hold secrets. They *read* one another. They *know* one another, backwards and forwards, thoroughly, purely, and share all things together.

God is not alone nor lonely. Neither is God sad nor empty. God is Triune—Father and Son existing in joyous relationship, real communion, fellowship of the highest order in the Spirit. We get a glimpse of this fellowship when we hear the Father declare to Jesus, "Thou art my beloved Son, in whom my soul delights!" and we hear Jesus answer, "*Abba!* Father!" This is powerful language.

It is certainly not cold or sterile. And it is far from being the kind of language that triggers hesitance, hiding or mere outward performance. Look at this again:

> Thou art my *beloved* Son, in whom my soul *delights!*
> *Abba!* Father!

This is the language of a full heart—of passion, acceptance and delight. It is the language of fellowship, of hurried inclusion, of embracing, of mutual adoration and real affection. It reveals a passionate, encircling love which generates freedom to be known and reaches expression in a communion of intimacy, familiarity and complete togetherness. While the old adage "familiarity breeds contempt" may well be true in certain situations, it is not true with God. What we see here is acceptance and love expressing itself in a communion of exquisitely thorough familiarity in the Spirit.

We have all experienced those moments when we found it very difficult to look another person in the eye. We could scan the face of the other and perhaps momentarily look at the other person's eyes, but then almost uncontrollably our eyes would dart away as if desperately trying to avoid a real connection. This is the fruit of being ashamed, of feeling wrong. It may be that we were in fact wrong. Or it may be that the other person had a way of making us feel wrong. Either way, we felt ashamed, our conscience was not clean, and it decidedly affected our freedom to be known. It made us reticent, guarded, self-conscious, "ill at ease," as we say. We stumbled for words and the conversation was anything but intimate and freeflowing.

"I am in my Father" means that God is not like this. The Father and Son do not have this problem. They do not look at one another in doubt or insecurity or with unspoken accusation. When the Father calls the name of his Son, Jesus does not bristle with fear, nor does shame sweep over his heart and transform him into a religious android. The calling of his name is an event of pure liberty in the Spirit. The Father and Son *belong* to one another and they live in the untold freedom of mutual acceptance, in the openness and free-flowing sharing of a clean conscience. Nothing is hidden, nothing is reserved, there is no self-consciousness, no dis-ease, no fear or hesitance. They live face to face, in the Spirit.

"Thou art my beloved!" "*Abba!* Father!" This language is telling us about an abounding fellowship of life, a fellowship of shameless freedom to know and be known, a fellowship of unqualified appreciation and unreserved embracing, of complete familiarity, self-exposure and sharing, so much so that the only way to even begin to describe this relationship is to say that the Father and Son are not only with one another but in one another. For there is no separation, no distance or withholding.

Now, all that we were saying about home in the first chapter, about belonging to another person, about the spontaneous, flourishing and thriving fellowship of being, about the *concert of life* birthed in the convergence of mutual summoning, is really a description of God. It is a description of this relationship between the Father and Son in the Spirit, of *their concert*. This is where the flourishing, thriving joy of belonging and the life of home exists. It is here in the relationship of the Father and Son in the Spirit, and nowhere else. And that little preposition "in," which Jesus uses and which seems so odd to us, is telling us about its sheer rightness, blessedness, wonder and glory and about its singularity and utter uniqueness.

But there is something else here that we dare not miss. When Jesus says, "I am in my Father," he is not speaking by remote control, or shouting down to us from a balcony on the edge of eternity. He is speaking to us as *one of us.* He is speaking to us out of the fact that he has become human. He is speaking as the *incarnate* Son. And he is telling us that he is in the Father as a human being. He is telling us that this Triune relationship now includes a human being.

It is not that Jesus has suddenly been adopted into this relationship from the outside, as if he was not already part of it. It is rather that what he has always enjoyed with his Father has now become human. The eternal relationship of the Father and Son in the Spirit has now been "earthed" as Jesus. It has taken shape inside human existence. It has been translated into human being. The rich and blessed fellowship of the Father and Son in the Spirit is now and forever a divine-human fellowship.

The Son has always been the apple of the Father's eye, eternally so, but now he is this as a human being. He knows his Father's singular affection, dwells in shameless freedom and mutual delight with Him, loves Him with all of his heart, soul, mind and strength and shares all things with Him, as always, but now as a *man.*

When Jesus says, "In that day you will know that I am in my Father," he is saying, "You will see that far from being dead, I am alive in real relationship with my Father. You will see that I belong to Him and He to me. You will see our togetherness, our concert, our home-life. You will see that I am not only *with* my Father but *in* Him. And you will see me there as a man, a human being!"

Two very important points are pressing upon us for recognition here. The first is the fact that God is a relational being, a God of communion, existing in a great fellowship of love. As the Bible says, "God is love" (I John 4:8), and love cannot exist without relationship. Love reaches full expression in acceptance and cherishing, in freedom to know and be known, and in the life of so knowing and being known—fellowship. And fellowship reaches its fulfillment in union, the complete absence of fear, hiding and withholding, and the presence of real togetherness, at-oneness and oneness, without loss of individual identity—perichoresis. God exists in this way, as the Triune God—Father, Son and Spirit—in a perichoretic fellowship of love.

The second point is the fact that nothing less than this divine fellowship of Father, Son and Spirit has set up shop, as it were, on earth and fulfilled itself inside human being and existence. The Triune life is no longer simply an eternal divine fellowship up there in heaven. It has now expressed itself in space and time, in human existence. Jesus Christ is the eternal Son of the Father. But he has now become human. He is, as always, the Father's beloved, the embraced, the one who knows and loves the Father and lives in real and joyous fellowship with Him in the Spirit—but he is all this now as a human being.

The astonishing reality that confronts us in the Christmas story is that this divine fellowship of Father, Son and Spirit, this divine society of love and communion, this divine life, has translated itself into human form. And with the Christmas story goes the equally staggering news of the Ascension, when the *incarnate* Son ascended into heaven and sat down at the right hand of God the

Father Almighty, as the Creed says. Mark well that it was neither an angel nor a ghost that rose from the grave and ascended to the Father. It was Jesus Christ, the *incarnate* Son. As a human being, never to disincarnate himself, he sits at the Father's right hand, the place of honor, privilege and glory. As a human being, he knows the Father, lives in His pleasure in the fellowship of the Spirit, and is in everything God is. Nothing less than this is what confronts us in the Christian message.

Why would Jesus do this? Why would he stoop to become human? He had no need of this. He has forever known his Father and enjoyed his Father's full attention and affection. He has forever shared the concert of life with his Father in the Spirit. Why would he take the time and pain of earthing this fellowship of life? Why would the Triune God do such a thing? Was it because of some deficiency in their fellowship? Was it because of boredom? Of course not! The only reason to earth and humanize this eternal home-life was to share it, with us. As one of the ancients put it, Jesus became "what we are that He might bring us to be even what He is Himself."[2] Is this not too good for words? Could God really be like this and have these designs on me, on us, on the world? From a Christian perspective, anything less than this God, and this picture of overflowing fellowship determined to include us, is simply a figment of our imaginations, an idol, a perverse deception!

"You in me." The second part of this statement now takes on a quite staggering meaning. He who is the apple of the Father's

---

2 St. Irenaeus, *Against the Heresies*, book V, preface, in *The Ante-Nicene Fathers*, vol. 1: *The Apostolic Fathers with Justin Martyr and Irenaeus*, ed. by Alexander Roberts and James Donaldson (Grand Rapids: Wm. B. Eerdmans Pub. Co, reprinted 1987)

eye, the beloved in whom the Father's soul delights, the embraced, the one who lives in real fellowship with his Father in the Spirit—this one—says, *"you in me!"* Is this not a breathtaking statement? Could three little words possibly be more amazing? Stop and take this in.

In the simplest of terms Jesus is telling us that we are included in *him*. On the one hand, he tells us of his remarkable relationship with his Father. On the other hand, he tells us that we are included in him in his relationship with his Father. *We* are included in *this* blessed circle of shared life.

"You in me," this means that with Jesus we come under the Father's glorious declaration, "Thou art my beloved Son, in whom my soul delights!" And it means that we have been gathered into Jesus' answer, *"Abba!* Father!" We have a place in *this* fellowship. This is home, our home.

Some years ago I was standing in an airport waiting to meet a friend coming to visit us in Scotland. While I was waiting for my friend's plane I could not help but notice a young man standing in the waiting area. He was obviously excited and anxious. He would nervously check the arrivals monitor and then pace a little, glance at the runway, and come back to the monitor again.

Before long a flight arrived and we could see the plane taxiing to the terminal. It was clear that this was the flight for which he had been waiting. He positioned himself directly in front of the doors to the corridors that go out to the planes. Before long the doors were opened and people of every kind began to emerge, some smiling, some with that "where do I go now" look on their faces, some eagerly looking for a familiar face.

Then it happened. A little boy emerged and stopped in the

doorway. He scanned the crowds. Like an alarmed deer he desperately strained to hear. Then he heard his dad's voice, their eyes met and the little boy dashed across the floor with every fiber of his being. It was an event. Everything in the airport seemed to stop. It was as if someone hit a huge pause button and the whole world stopped to watch this little boy and his dad.

In the twinkling of an eye the little boy sprang from the doorway to his dad and jumped into his arms. No parent could have seen this without tears. It was a moment of embrace in undiluted joy, sheer delight and togetherness.

The very instant I saw this boy and his dad embrace, it was as though a voice from heaven called out:

> Baxter, Baxter, there is the gospel, there it is before your eyes. There is the resurrection and ascension of my beloved incarnate Son. There he is, coming, as man, with all haste to Me from the far country. There is our embrace. And the good news is, he is not alone, he has you and the world with him.

Nothing less than this is what Jesus is telling us in those three wonderful words, "you in Me." He is in the Father. He alone has this relationship with God, this right relationship with his Father, this spontaneous, free-flowing togetherness in the Spirit, but he is not alone—we are included in him. He has a home with God the Father Almighty and we are included.

We have to look at the life of Jesus Christ two different times. The first time we are preoccupied with the astonishing fact of the incarnation. The eternal Son of the Father became human. And in his incarnate existence, he fleshed out, expressed, fulfilled his eternal home-life with his Father in a human way. In the first instance, all our attention is upon what happened to the Son of God, what became of him in the incarnation. We see him die, rise again and ascend to his Father. And we see him now, as the incarnate, crucified and risen Son, home with his Father in the fellowship of the Spirit.

But then we must look a second time at the life of Jesus Christ. This time we see that in his life, death, resurrection and ascension something was happening to us. When he died, we died (2 COR 5:14). In his incarnate life, the Triune God was doing something to you, me and the world. "God was in Christ reconciling the world to Himself" (2 COR 5:19). From the one side, we see that Jesus Christ is the incarnate Son living out his relationship with his Father as a human being. From the other side, we see that Jesus Christ is the act of the Triune God by which we were taken, cleansed and included in the blessed circle. The early church thought of Jesus and the Spirit along these lines, as the two arms of the Father by which He reached down to us, laid hold of us, cleansed us and brought us home.

In Jesus Christ, the Triune God laid hold of Adam, you, me, the world, and in his death, Adam died, you died, we all died. In his death we were crucified. By his death we were circumcised, radically cleansed of all sin and alienation, wholly converted. By his resurrection, we were brought forth as new, alive, without spot or wrinkle. And his ascension was the act by which we were taken to the Father, ushered into His presence and established in real relationship with Him.

In the first instance, our attention is focused upon what became of the Son in his incarnation-ascension. In the second instance, it is focused upon what became of us in him. For the whole event of Jesus' coming—his life, death, resurrection and ascension—was a vicarious event. It was an event in which we were decisively implicated. It was an event in which God dealt with us.

This is the point for us to see: In Jesus, the Triune God not only did something *for* us, but did something *with* and *to* us. The life of Jesus Christ is the act of the Father absolutely refusing to forsake us, refusing to leave us floundering in alienation, refusing to leave us excluded from the circle of life. His life is the act of the Father's passion for us reaching across every chasm, breaking through every barrier, relentlessly searching us out and finding us, laying hold of us and bringing us home.

Jesus says, "I am in my Father, and you in me." This simple statement is a summary of what Jesus Christ accomplished in his coming. On the one hand, he humanized his eternal home-life with his Father in the Spirit. On the other hand, he laid hold of us, removed our alienation in his death, brought us forth new in his resurrection and exalted us into the Father's presence and fellowship in his ascension.

Herein lies the deepest truth about us. We are included in the incarnate Son's existence with his Father. We have been given a place in *this* relationship. And just as it is a flagrant violation of the very nature of the fellowship of Father, Son and Spirit to say merely that they are three, so it is a grievous violation of what the Triune God has done with us in Jesus Christ, to see ourselves as alone, forsaken, ashamed, wrong! For we are *in him* who is in the Father. We are home.

Staggering and startling as it is, it remains the great truth about us. It is the secret of our existence. It may be veiled to us, hidden from our sight and very far removed from the way we see ourselves and our lives; nevertheless, it is true. The eternal Son became human. As a human being he knows his Father inside and out, and dwells in faithfulness and security, joy and freedom with his Father in the Spirit. And we have been included in his incarnate relationship with his Father. We *are* included.

"I in you." We have covered a fair amount of territory, have we not? We have moved from an interest in the mysterious power of the word *home* to the rich togetherness and concert of the Triune God. And we have begun to grapple with the startling double-truth that (a) this divine concert has reached expression in human being, and (b) we have been and are included in it. This double-truth sets before us our true identity, our true home.

But there is a third point, which goes beyond our identity, and sets before us the very secret of our existence. Perhaps we should say, it brings out the implications of our true identity in Christ. The last three words in Jesus' statement (I in you) confront us with the fact that life as we know it now, your life, my life, is much more than we ever imagined. There is a factor in the equation of our living that has eluded us completely—Jesus Christ is not somewhere up there in his Father, he is in us. His relationship with his Father in the fellowship of the Spirit is not quarantined to some heavenly warehouse in the far corners of the universe; it is at work within us now expressing itself in our humanity. This is the mystery of our lives. We are participants in Jesus' home-life with his Father.

When my own son was about six years old, he and one of his buddies strolled into our den, where I was sitting sorting through mail. I did not know his friend at all. We were strangers. But what happened is a fascinating illustration of the mystery at work within us. While this little boy did not know me or what I was like, my son did. My son had a relationship with me. He was at-home with me and free to be frivolous, free to come into my presence and play. And he did just this. In the freedom of acceptance he sauntered into my presence, bounced on the couch, and engaged me in play. And his friend found himself in the presence of something that was not his. He found himself encircled by and in the midst of our fellowship. My son's freedom and at-homeness with me worked its way into that little boy's heart. He experienced it. He played in it and it became his too.

This is a picture of the mystery of our existence. This is what is going on in our lives now. In sheer grace, we have been included in the incarnate Son's home-life with his Father, and all that is bound up in this relationship is at work within us. We are living in it, walking around in it, breathing Christological air, participating in Christ's connection with God's existence, and sharing in his experience of home.

Jesus Christ alone knows the Father and has a real and right relationship with Him (MT 11:27). He alone knows the acceptance of God the Father Almighty, shares in the dignity, glory, joy and security of the Father, experiences His pleasure and delight, and lives in the fellowship of life with Him in the Spirit. But he has chosen not to be alone. He has chosen to share himself with us. He is giving us a share in his existence and in what he sees and knows and experiences when he looks God the Father in the eyes. He is sharing with us his at-homeness, his freedom from hiding and freedom for fellowship with his Father. We are caught up in his relationship with his Father and it is expressing itself in our humanity, in our hearts, thoughts, actions and relationships.

Herein lies the fundamental difference between religion and Christianity. Religion does not know about Christmas. It does not know about the incarnation of the Son or the humanization of his eternal home-life with his Father in the Spirit. Religion does not know that we have been included in this relationship. It does not know about the presence of *this* Jesus Christ in our lives, hearts, thoughts and relationships now—this Jesus who knows his Father, loves Him with all his heart, soul, mind and strength, enjoys the delight and pleasure of the Father, and glories in all that He has made.

The religious man thus sees himself standing on his own, as a pure individual. He does not see himself as a participant in the heart and knowing of Jesus Christ. He has his own heart and mind irrespective of any other. He is thus left to himself to glorify God. And he is left with the prideful conclusion that his interest in things divine, his concern for justice, his caring for others, his basic goodness, his yearnings and prayers, his fellowship with friends and his love for family and life all have their origin in his own heart. Or he is left under the eventually debilitating assumption that he must produce all these things in and of himself. Religion has no mediator. It leaves humanity standing on its own before God.

Christianity is not religion. Christianity is about the home-life that Jesus Christ has with his Father in the Spirit expressing itself in and through us, taking shape in us as work, play, cooking and cleaning, as fishing, golfing and gardening, as fellowship, relationships, friendships and marriages. Christianity is about nothing less than the life of Jesus Christ being formed in us (GAL 4:19; EPH 4:13). It is about the humanity of the Triune God filling all things (EPH 4:10).

From one angle, this is the goal toward which creation moves and for which we pray (EPH 3:14-19; JN 17:22-26). We pray for the kingdom to come, and what is the kingdom of God but the home-life, the joy, the security and freedom, the love and fellowship which the incarnate Son has now and forever in his relationship with his Father in the Spirit? What is the coming of the kingdom but the life of this Jesus filling us and all creation? Isn't this home? Isn't this our deepest desire, the longing prayer within us?

But from another angle, we must see that this is not a goal at all but a very present reality. "I in you" means that we are now caught up in and participating in Jesus Christ. He is in us now, sharing himself with us and expressing himself through us. His home-life, his joys and burdens, his delights and freedom, his security and assurance, his hope and peace are already at work in you. This is the secret, the mystery that is so close to us that we cannot see it.

It is not our fellowship that we enjoy. It is not our hunger or thirsting for justice. It is not our goodness or burdens for others. It is not our pleasure in the sunset, not our passion for life or our freedom to play. It is not our interest in deeper things or our longing to be real. It is not our groaning cry to know and be known. It is not our security that sets us free to run. It is Jesus Christ in us. It is the fellowship of the Father's "Thou art Mine!" and the incarnate Son's "*Abba*, Father!" forming itself and expressing itself in us in the Spirit. But we are so deceived we cannot see it. It is all too human, too normal, too close. We look past it all to busy ourselves with other things.

Jesus says, "Apart from Me, you can do nothing" (JN 15:5). How do we understand this "nothing"? Does it literally mean "nothing"? Does it mean that apart from Jesus we cannot even breathe, laugh, delight in food and friends, love our children, play basketball? Or does "nothing" mean more lofty things like praying, reading the Bible, going to church, witnessing?

For years I have struggled with Paul's statement about the witness of the Spirit in our hearts: "And because you are sons, God has sent forth the Spirit of His Son into our hearts, crying, 'Abba, Father!'" Who doesn't want to experience all that this witness means? But for me, it always seemed such a lofty thing, so enigmatic and mysterious, so super spiritual. It was way up there, above and beyond me. "Maybe one day," I would say to myself, "I will make it to this level."

Then one day it hit me like a bolt from the blue: Baxter, do you think that on your own you would actually care about such things? Do you honestly think that on your own you would have moved beyond the Lion's fearful and quick exit, when he finally faced the great Wizard with Dorothy, in the *Wizard of Oz*? Do you think that on your own you would have any passion to study, reflect and wrestle, let alone a clean conscience and actual freedom to approach God in prayer? Where did *you* get a clean conscience? From where have you derived this bold freedom to approach God and call Him "Father"? Do these things have their origin in your heart?

No. It is Jesus' *Abba* already at work in you, expressing itself in your mind and heart and life. It is his relationship, his interest and love for his Father, his freedom and fellowship with his Father already at work in you in the Spirit, being formed in you. It is not you, but Christ in you.

What must the Lord think of us as we gather to have our grand meetings to worship and glorify Him? We pray that He would come and be present and that He would accept our worship. As if He were absent. As if we, on our own, because of our own hearts, actually desired to worship Him. As if we, on our own, apart from Jesus Christ's relationship with his Father, apart from his love and delight in his Father, apart from his at-homeness and clean conscience, apart from his passion to know and honor his Father, would gather at all, let alone produce something of consequence for God's glory. What pride! What blind and stifling ignorance! The kingdom of God is indeed already here.

But what about the rest of our lives? What about Monday through Saturday? What about our work and our play? What about our delights in music and fellowship? What about our interest in the universe or the whales, the plants? What about our concerns for the broken and sick? What about our romance and our pleasure in the glory of the day? What about our freedom to rest, that marvelous security at work within us that actually allows us to close our eyes and let go? What about our sacrifice for the good of others? From whence does all of this come? Does it originate in our hearts? Does it have its source in our goodness? Is it our love and delight and joy and burden? No. It is Jesus Christ in us, the hope of glory (COL 1:27), for apart from him we can do nothing.

"I in you" means that there is much more going on within us and around us than we ever imagined. The very faith and faithfulness of Jesus Christ, his joy and assurance, his security and hope, his freedom and clean conscience, his unashamedness and free-flowing fellowship with his Father are expressing themselves in our lives. This is not a goal; it is happening. We are the fruit of his mediation.

Isn't this what we love in life, in music, in the beauty of the sunset, in our relationships, in our work and play? Our glory in Jesus Christ, our place in the Father's delight and affection for Jesus, the unforced rhythm of the Father's acceptance, the flourishing, thriving joy of Jesus' belonging, express their reality in us, we share in them, we know the concert for ourselves.

Isn't this the real source of the inconsolable dream? In Jesus we have a home with God the Father Almighty. We know its joy and life and flourishing. We have tasted its glory. We have heard the music and known the dance. But we are not satisfied. Something hinders our participation. We are not free for full participation in Jesus' fellowship with his Father. And our true home in Jesus Christ, the mystery, *beckons*. It will not go away. It is the most profound and searching and gnawing desire within us. *Homesickness!*

Isn't this the real power of the word home for us? It is the particular configuration of letters that we have come to associate with this flourishing life when our participation in the Triune concert was let loose to be itself in us.

Home gathers such a brood of nuances, speaks volumes to us, almost magically haunts us, goads us and inspires us, because it is the physical and audible symbol of all that the mystery of our inclusion in Christ means to us. The word *home* reminds us of what we know in our souls—there is indeed such a relationship of glory, such a home life, such a concert; we are included in it and belong to it, have a place in it; and while we have experienced it, tasted it and felt it, we have yet to be baptized in it.

CHAPTER 3

The Way Home

In the statement of Jesus that has been occupying our thought, we are confronted with a startling and wonderful vision of human existence and life. Central to this vision is the incarnation of the eternal Son of God. We must not think of the incarnation as being only a temporary mode, a form that Jesus assumed for a moment in the past. His humanity is not a robe which he put on for a while but has now taken off and put away in a heavenly closet. The miracle of Christmas is that the Son of God *became* human. The miracle of the ascension is that he *continues* to be human. He sits now, as a human being, at the Father's right hand, knowing his Father and sharing all things with Him in the fellowship of the Spirit.

But this is only the beginning of the vision. Jesus goes on to say that we are included. He is the vicarious man, the *one* in whom *we* were gathered, cleansed and given a real relationship with the Father. The incarnation-ascension of the Son is the act in and through which we were crucified, circumcised and reconciled, brought forth anew and exalted to the Father. Jesus Christ is our home with the Father.

But even here the vision is not complete. For we are not only included in Jesus' relationship with his Father, but that relationship—that home-life—is expressing itself in us now. Jesus—and his home-life with his Father—is not up there in ome ethereal world; he is in us. We are participants in his sonship.

It is not that we exist by some undefined creative grace of God, in addition to which we then share in Jesus' life with the Father. Jesus *is* the mediator between the life of the Triune God and humanity. We exist, we have being and life, because he is in the Father, because he is connected with the existence and being of God, and he is sharing this existence and being with us. Descartes' famous dictum, "I think, therefore I am," is wrong. It should be, "Jesus Christ is in the Father, therefore I am."

But our participation in Christ is more than merely a matter of existence, as if we have our existence through Christ but then are on our own to form that existence and give it character. We are more than animals ruled by our instincts. We are persons who have dignity and joy in our labors, hope and peace in our hearts, a sense of security which liberates us from the tyranny of fear, a delight in life, a concern for the planet and its welfare. But these things do not have their origin in our good hearts. They have their origin in Jesus Christ, first, because he shares in the Father's glory and dignity, in His security, assurance and joy, and in His delight and passion for His creation; and second, because this Jesus Christ is sharing himself, not just his existence but all he is and has with his Father, with us.

It is because Jesus knows the Father and the freedom of the Father's complete acceptance, and because he shares his mind and knowing with us, that we are not utterly debilitated by guilt and shame. While he alone among human beings has a clean conscience, he shares his clean conscience with us, and therefore we are not bound into complete and fearful hiding from God and from one another, but free for fellowship, free to give ourselves for and to others. Because he knows the absolute security of the Father's embrace, and because he shares his mind with us, we know freedom to rest and relax, freedom to be still and notice the glory all around us, freedom to sleep in expectation of a good tomorrow. The mystery of our existence and life is that we are participants in his incarnate and ascended sonship. He is the mediator. We are the fruit of his home-life with his Father.

Yet all of this is qualified in our hearts by a serious "yes, but." Yes, this is true, but it is also not true. There are times when it seems to be more true than others. There are times, many times—days, months and even years—when we cannot rest or relax, when we find ourselves so driven we never get close to noticing the glory, let alone enjoying it. There are times when we cannot sleep at all. There are times when there is no joy or dignity or meaning in our labors, when fear and anxiety overwhelm us, when we play but are not playing at all, when we are present with others but far from free to know or be known, in fact seemingly bound to pretense and deceit, camouflage and self-protection—even driven to slander, oppression and brutality.

A strange and gross mixture is at work within us, a mixture of fear and freedom, joy and depression, peace and angst, a mixture of rest and fretfulness, fellowship and hiding, service and self-centeredness, love and hate. We know both home and homelessness at the same time. Clearly there is another factor in the equation of our lives besides that of Jesus Christ and his home-life with his Father in the Spirit. There is something that hinders and stifles and suffocates the life of Christ within us, even perverts it.

The problem is twofold. On the one side, the stifling of Christ's life in us is the result of our unbelief. On the other side, the problem of our unbelief is the result of deception. While it certainly seems trite to say that the problem is that we do not believe the truth of who we are in Christ, there is far more to this statement than first appears. To begin with, we give ourselves to the things we believe in, to those things we believe will ultimately give us life, wholeness, fullness. But, as the Bible says, we are confused. We see through a darkened pair of glasses (ICOR 13:12). Our vision is clouded, blurred. Our thinking and understanding are skewed and darkened.

In our confusion, we give ourselves willingly and freely to thoughts and actions which stifle the sonship of Jesus Christ at work within us. In our darkness, we embrace things, even run to them, that smother our participation in his life and fellowship with his Father. In our skewed thinking, we believe in the wrong things, pursue them, give ourselves over to them, and our life in Christ cannot reach proper expression in us. We actually turn from Jesus Christ and walk after emptiness, and we become empty (JER 2:4). In our confusion, we misunderstand the source of the living water in us and we set about to hew cisterns for ourselves, broken cisterns that hold no water (JER 2:13), and we become parched.

Jesus says that knowing the truth sets us free (JN 8:32). The reverse of this statement is also true—not knowing the truth binds us. Not knowing the truth, being in the dark, leads us, or better yet, *misleads* us, to believe in the wrong thing and thus give ourselves over to things that keep the life and glory of Jesus Christ from flowering fully in us.

Jesus Christ has included us in his belonging and flourishing relationship with his Father. He has involved us and made us participants in his existence and home-life. Without him we would not exist and we would have no good at all, no burdens or passions or interests, no creativity or talent, no hope, no security, no actual freedom, and not the least semblance of joy and life. But we are not without him and thus every step we take is a Christological step, a possibility created by the fact that he mediates existence to us, bathes our souls in his security and hope and shares with us his concerns and talents. But we are far from knowing this as the way things are. We do not see ourselves in Jesus Christ and we do not know that Jesus Christ is in us. And even in those rare cases when we do think about Christ in us, it is a vague and mystical notion that we cannot really grasp, and the Jesus that we think about is rather boring and inept, far from the beloved Son of the Father who lives, as man, in his Father's fellowship and dignity and joy in the Holy Spirit. We are confused, and our confusion is disastrous because it leaves us believing and embracing a false view of ourselves and a false view of the source and secret of life.

A few nights ago my two daughters and I read together. There were thirty stuffed animals, three persons and one book. "Isn't this the greatest thing in all the world?" I asked them. "The Lord loves us so much that He gives us a share in the joy He has in His Son—He puts it in us through His Spirit and we get to experience it together."

Later I pondered over how confused we get about this. How long will it take us to see that what we shared in has little to do with Daddy per se, with teddy bears and books, or with the event of reading together? How long will it take us to understand that what happened then was not our creation but the event of the Spirit, not the fruit of our goodness but the fruit of Jesus Christ's presence and self-giving?

We are in him and he is in us. We share in his humanity and home-life with his Father. But we get Jesus Christ confused with ourselves and his home-life confused with the outer form by which it expresses itself in our lives. We do not know of the presence of Jesus Christ. We do not understand that it is his home-life and fellowship with his Father, his security and joy, that is at work within us in the Spirit. Confused about this great fact, we assume that the life comes from elsewhere. Perhaps it came from us. Perhaps we produced it. Perhaps the secret lies in the outer form of its expression, i.e., in teddy bears, books and reading together. Thus, with all that we have, we desperately try to get the recipe just right again. So we pour ourselves and our time and energy into the mechanical recreation of the outer form. In our confusion we pursue things which have no actual substance in themselves, and the good and glorious life of Jesus Christ in us is suffocated.

Is this not the story of our lives—one confused attempt after another to find home for ourselves, to create it, manufacture it, conjure it up by our own resources? We try to find it in marriage, in friendships, in our children, in our pets, in our careers or work, in our glamour and glory, in our emotions and feelings, in sensuality and sex, in our noble causes and clubs, in our profound academics, in our athletics and recreation, in our material possessions, in our politics and power, in church or the Bible or our religious doings, in our chants and crystals. But the home-life of Jesus Christ with his Father is not in any of these.

The experience of home does not come by believing in any of these things and thus pursuing them as goals or ends in themselves. It is true, wonderfully true, that our participation in the home-life of the Triune God expresses itself in and takes the form of fellowship, marriage, friendship, service, work, study and play. That is the way it is supposed to be. We are supposed to fish, play golf and garden in Jesus' freedom and joy. We are supposed to share in the fellowship of Jesus Christ with friends and family. We are supposed to live with ourselves, with others and with creation in the security, hope and peace of Jesus Christ. We are supposed to work as participants in his dignity and meaning. But in and of themselves, these things—relationships, work and play—are powerless. They are empty. They do not possess the concert and cannot even play real music. In and of themselves they have nothing to give to us.

Home exists in one place only—in Jesus' relationship with his Father in the Spirit. And he shares his life with us, but we confuse the source with its expression; the fellowship of the Father and Son in the Spirit with the forms it takes in our lives; home with places, people and things. We get so confused we make little idols out of each of them. We seek them, believe in them, honor them and give ourselves to them assuming that they can become home for us. We become golfaholics and workaholics, religious addicts, slaves of money, sex and power. We prostrate ourselves before the system. Why? Because we are confused about the source and secret of our true life and we believe that one or another of these things will give true life to us. The emptiness of these idols is like a huge black hole which sucks the life of Christ out of us. And we become black holes as well. For in our desperation to experience home, we turn to one another and demand from each other the reality of home which none of us possess in ourseves. We all but destroy each other demanding the life we do not have to give.

It has been several years since the movie *Chariots of Fire* was released. But it has some rather unforgettable scenes. One such scene happened just after Harold Abrahams won the 100-yard dash in the 1924 Olympic games. He had worked so hard and against such odds. He had raced against such champions. And he had won. He had won! But there he was with his revered coach, plunged into a drunken stupor. The form had no glory to give him, no real glory. He had pursued it with all of his might, grabbed hold of it and now possessed it. He held the medal in his hands. He was the fastest man on earth. But it was only the form of glory, and the pain of its emptiness was unbearable, it had to be numbed.

What a contrast Abrahams was to Eric Liddel, the flying Scotsman. Who can forget that scene under the mountain in Edinburgh when Liddel spoke to his sister? He said, "God made me fast, and when I run I feel *His pleasure*." Running, winning, being an Olympic champion were for Liddel but the mere expression of participation in the delight of the Father in His Son. Running was but the outer form of the event of the Spirit, the expression of the concert of the Father's pleasure. How wonderfully free he was to move on from running to other, seemingly less noble, forms of participation. But for Liddel, it was all of a piece. It was participation in the pleasure of the Father in His Son, whether in racing for Olympic gold, shoveling mud or suffering persecution on the mission field.

Most of us are not like Eric Liddel. We are like Harold Abrahams. We believe that the forms actually have what we long for and we give ourselves over to pursue them. How pitifully shallow and ghostly we become in their pursuit. How angry and frustrated, depressed and bitter we become when the promising forms seem forever out of our reach and beyond our possession. How close we teeter on the edge of pure despair and cynicism when we manage to grab hold of one of the forms and then begin to see that there is nothing in it. What a grievous and dreadful pain it is to see through the thing in which we have invested such hope and time and energy.

Confusion and unbelief towards Jesus Christ lead us to believe in the wrong things, and as we give ourselves to pursue them, they suffocate and stifle the good life of Jesus Christ in us. But there is another factor in the equation of our confusion which needs now to be brought into our discussion. Our confusion and darkness do not have their ultimate origin in us. Behind all of our confusion is Diabolos—the devil, satan, the evil one. He is the spirit of error as the Scripture testifies—the author of confusion, the father of lies, the accuser, the enemy, the one who opposes our participation in the life of the Triune God. Darkness and confusion and idolatry and emptiness originate not with us, but with him.

The evil one is not a creator. He cannot speak things into existence as did the Triune God. He does not possess that kind of power. He cannot create an alternate universe, kingdom or humanity. There are thus not two creations, or two humanities, existing side by side, the one being the creation of the Triune God and the other being the creation of the devil. There is only the one creation of the Triune God. There is only the one humanity, created and redeemed in Jesus Christ, given the gift of participation in his incarnate and ascended life and fellowship with his Father in the Spirit.

The fact that the evil one does not have creative power means that the only way he can bring his dream—his scheme of a rival kingdom—to form is by exploiting the creation of the Triune God to his own ends. He has no power to create his own world nor to sustain it. He thus operates parasitically: he uses and misuses the creation of the Triune God for his own purpose. He misuses the life of Jesus Christ in us.

His chief, and perhaps only, weapon is confusion. He confuses us about our reality in Jesus Christ, spreads lies and misinformation about Jesus and us, so that we do not know the truth of who we are—beloved, accepted, reconciled, justified, embraced and adopted by God the Father Almighty in Jesus Christ, included in the circle of the Triune life. And confusion about who we are in Jesus Christ means that we believe that we are not beloved, not acceptable, not reconciled, not justified, not embraced, not adopted. Confusion only means that we believe that we are not included in the circle of life that Jesus shares with his Father in the Spirit, that we are lost, empty, alone. And it is impossible for us to sit still in this state of affairs. In fact, not a single one of us is sitting still. We are in hot pursuit of that thing which we believe will make us beloved, found, acceptable, full, home. Or we have reached the conclusion that it is all impossible and have become angry, frustrated, depressed and despairing cynics.

The eclipse of our true identity as joint heirs with Jesus Christ in his life with his Father leaves us irresistibly vulnerable to every dazzling suggestion of the deceiver. "What thou seekest is here. It is in this person, this job, this achievement, this amount of money, in this church, in this religion, this club, this adventure, this trip, this house, this relationship." And off we go personally and corporately into bondage, into the headlong pursuit of our secret idols, those things we believe will give us identity, meaning and life. We run to embrace them and they are empty, and even when we begin to suspect that they are empty, we get up and embrace them again. For there is nothing else, or so it seems.

The good and glorious life of Jesus Christ in us, his peace and joy, his flourishing freedom, are thereby suffocated. But even more than this, his good and glorious life in us is thereby misused, parasitically exploited, to produce chaos—wrath, anger, malice, greed, lust, slander, jealously, hatred, anxiety.

The tactic of the evil one is simple: Blind human beings to their truth in Jesus Christ, darken their understanding and confuse their spiritual perception of their true identity. "For if they do not know their true identity in Christ, they will be driven to find one somewhere else. Once they misunderstand the source and secret of their existence in Christ, they automatically think that they come from elsewhere—that home-life is in people, position, things, events. Then we have them. Like a martin to a gourd they will follow every promise we set before them. And they will be left utterly empty, miserable, broken, devastated."

The answer, the way home, is, as the Bible insists, *faith* in Jesus Christ. There are no secret buttons to push, no magical elixirs to take, no special potions, no chants to recite or charms to handle.

There are no decoder rings or esoteric theological classes to take and no mechanical principles to apply to our lives. It is not a matter of church membership, water baptism or being religious. The answer is faith—and faith means unconfusion, seeing clearly, discovering and knowing reality in Christ, embracing it, acknowledging it, loving it—responding to Jesus Christ with a serious and hearty and continuous "*Amen!*"

Faith in Jesus Christ means faith in the fact that he is in the Father, that he has a real and right relationship with God the Father Almighty. It means faith in the fact that he has included me in this relationship. And it means faith in the fact that I am a participant in his life, that he is my Lord, savior, salvation, my life, my home. And faith in this Jesus—not the religious Jesus of the icons or the impotent Jesus of the modern Church, but the Jesus in whom we have a real relationship with the Father—faith in this Jesus produces freedom for life. To believe in this Jesus means that we no longer see ourselves as lost, but found; that we no longer believe ourselves to be alienated or empty, but reconciled and filled. And this faith produces not hopelessness or anger, not lust or greed or neediness, but peace, confidence, security and joy.

To believe in this Jesus means that we believe ourselves to be known, accepted and cherished by the Father Himself. And what happens to us and in us when we encounter such Divine acceptance? What happens in us when we believe ourselves to be at-home with the Father? Are we plunged into bondage? Are we overwhelmed with fear and anxiety? Are we turned into religious androids? Do we become workaholics, materialists, sexual addicts, murderers, gossips? Are we enslaved to the crowd? No. We find ourselves released, set free from the very things that enslaved us.

We find a new freedom from the tyranny of work and greed and lust, a new freedom from the need for the approval of peers. We find ourselves at peace and playing golf in the kingdom, filled with joy and hope, free to look into our daughters' souls and share life with them, free to rest, free to love, free to be who we are. We find ourselves flourishing.

The problem for us is that we have been deceived, and we believe the deception. We believe that we are homeless, and therefore we are driven to find home. We continue to embrace the wrong thing, and thus stifle the life we have in Jesus Christ. Our thinking and understanding must undergo a radical change. Our darkened believing must be enlightened. We must be weaned from our faith in ourselves, other persons, things and ideas.

If this were the end of the story, it would be a sad state of affairs, for we would be left to ourselves to escape the deception of one who is far more powerful than we. But mark well that it could never be so. This world belongs to the Holy Trinity, created, reconciled and given the staggering gift of participation in the Triune life of God. This God is on the move, relentlessly and passionately at work in every quarter of the creation, warring against the deceiver, patiently educating our souls, exposing our false believing and our stifling, deadening service to idols, that we may know the truth, so that the life of Jesus Christ may flower into unencumbered fullness in us.

Jesus Christ is not only the mediator of existence and life; he is the true witness, the great prophet and evangelist, the good shepherd. He sees our false believing, our idolatry and bondage to nothingness. He sees our confusion and the parasitic and dastardly exploitation of his glorious life in us. He knows that we are not free to forsake our idols until we see the truth that he is our home. He knows that we are powerless to enlighten ourselves. It is his battle. And he is no reluctant warrior. Neither is he ill-equipped to do battle. He engages us in the Holy Spirit in a life-long process of spiritual enlightenment.

This is the real story of our lives now. From one side we can see our life as one confused attempt after another to manufacture *home* for ourselves. But from the other side, our life now is the process by which Jesus Christ strives with us in our darkness, enlightening our perception, so that we can see that he is our home. History, both personal and corporate, is about spiritual education. Jesus Christ is educating us in the Spirit. He is bringing us to know that he is our true home, so that we can see that he is what we are really after, to the end that we may freely and willingly forsake every dazzling pretender and embrace him with all of our hearts.

If you have ever written a poem or an essay or even a long letter, then you have a ready-made illustration of this process of enlightenment under Jesus Christ. A poet sits at her desk and wrestles to articulate an insight. Time after time she jerks the paper out of the typewriter, wads it up and trashes it, discontent with the particular form of expression. Again and again this happens until the expression is right. But why? Or, perhaps more accurately, how can this process happen? Who told her that this or that phrase was not quite right? Who told her to start again? How does she know that what she just wrote is in fact not the way to say it? How does she know when it is just right?

There is a deeper knowledge at work here, a spiritual knowledge far more real than the poem itself. This deeper, spiritual knowledge engages the mind, setting before it a vision which demands to be articulated. It guides and leads the mind, scrutinizing and evaluating each thought and turn of phrase. And it rejoices when the mind begins to comprehend and see the light. It lauds and honors the turn of phrase that brings it to verbal form.

Now, take this image of the poetic process and think of it in terms of your own life, stretch it out over eighty or so years and you have it. Jesus Christ is the deeper knowledge at work within each of us. In the secrecy and invisibility of the Spirit he sets a vision of home before us. He gives us a glimpse of who we really are. And what happens then? Do we walk away and go on about our business? No. The inconsolable dream is born. We spend the rest of our lives homesick, moving from one thing to the next in the frantic search for our true home. As Augustine said long ago: "Thou hast made us for Thyself and our hearts are restless till they rest in Thee."[3]

This is what is happening in each of us. We have a home in Jesus Christ. We are participants in his life and glory. But we are profoundly confused and unwittingly work against our own life. But Jesus Christ is the Word of God. He continually and inescapably addresses us in the truth.

The revelation of our home in Jesus scrutinizes and judges us. It penetrates our facades and exposes what we are desperately trying to call "glory" and laud and extol as "the good life" as being empty and boring, only a shadow of real glory and goodness. It tells us there is more, much more, that we are more.

The revelation of the fact that we have a home in Jesus Christ translates into gnawing dissatisfaction with the *status quo*, into

---

3 *The Confessions of St. Augustine*, translated by F. J. Sheed (London: Sheed and Ward, ninth impression, 1978), book I.i.38

a deep malcontentedness with mere existence, and engages us in a quiet but relentless quest for completion. How can you be content with fleeting human accolades when you have heard the news of your adoption by God the Father Almighty? You cannot. You are not.

What is the uneasiness we feel in life, the disturbance, the sense of being scrutinized? Why is it that playing golf has suddenly become boring? Why is it that working for money has become meaningless, that marriage, the hard-earned degree, the lost weight, the vacation, the church, has not really done for us what we hoped? Why is it that the sexual affair is now unfulfilling? Why has the emptiness of mere polite conversation become so acutely apparent? It is because Jesus Christ, the Word of God, has addressed you and you have tasted your glory and dignity and fellowship with God the Father Almighty in him. You have known home.

Jesus Christ points his finger only to liberate us from the things that are stifling the life of home in us. His purpose is not to take golf away from us, or marriage, study, health, rest or excitement. His purpose is to give them to us in fullness. But we are confused, and thus his scrutiny is designed to enlighten us, to unconfuse us, to lead us out of *faith in ourselves*, out of *faith in things*, into *faith in Christ* so that our participation in his life and knowing may be unhindered. These moments of crisis are designed to make us *unbelievers*, to help us see that there is nothing in the thing we are pursuing—that it is an empty well and has no living water—so that we can stop believing and hoping in it, stop giving ourselves over to it as an end in itself, stop drinking its emptiness. They are designed to help us discern that Jesus Christ is the living water in us, that we may *believe* in him and thus experience the undamming of the river. They are a call to retreat from idolatry so that we can have the full knowledge and life of the true God—Father and Son alive in the fellowship of the Spirit. These spiritual crises are the way home, basic training in proper faith.

Jesus Christ is our patient and determined Lord and Saviour. He is our true home refusing to allow us to flounder in the homelessness of confusion. He does not go away after a few crises and wrong decisions on our part. He comes again. He continues to reveal the truth to us in the Spirit. And each time the revelation cuts like a surgeon's knife because it is so exquisitely personal. It reveals our real glory, our real joy, our real home to us, and thus unmistakably reveals our blindness and ignorance, the wrongness of our present investments, the falsehood of our present believing, the waywardness of our hopes. Each time we are warned, seriously warned. Each time we are summoned to turn away from our confusion to embrace the truth in Jesus—to acknowledge who he is and who we are in him, to receive it, *amen* it.

Jesus Christ alone knows the Father. He alone knows the peace and dignity of the Father's embrace. He alone knows the flourishing, thriving joy of belonging to God the Father Almighty. He alone knows *home*. What is happening within us now is that the startling, wonderful fact that he has included us in his home with his Father in the Spirit is seizing our attention, engaging us personally, working within us to liberate us from serious and dastardly confusion that we may experience our inclusion fully. We are in spiritual school. We are under the tutelage of reality in Jesus Christ. We are being educated, delivered from evil.

Day by day Jesus Christ makes sure we know that we are included. Day by day he makes sure we know that we have a home in him. He encounters us. He gives himself—his knowing, his joy, peace and fellowship—to us. We know him, and the inconsolable dream is born. The search is on. Every confusion, every wrong turn, every misgiving are patiently and faithfully revealed for what they are and are not. Again and again he brings us to the crisis point, places us at a fork in the road of our believing and bids us to retreat from idolatry and acknowledge the true God, the Triune God, in whom we move and live and have our being. Again and again he brings us under the command of the truth, where we have no choice but to decide either to continue in our confusion and perish or to embrace the light and flourish.

For he is our merciful and faithful Lord and Saviour, the one Word of God forever addressing us in the Spirit that we may be delivered from confusion and come to know the truth, and thus experience baptism into the concert of the Triune God. He is the one Word of God forever encountering us, that the reality of our inclusion in the flourishing, thriving joy of his belonging, our inclusion in the sheer delight of the Father in His Son, our inclusion in their shameless, free flowing communion in the Spirit may flower into unencumbered expression in us, and we may know *home*.

Other Books by
C. Baxter Kruger

Patmos:
Three Days, Two Men
One Extraordinary Conversation

When Aidan finds himself far from his native Mississippi, he inexplicably meets the Apostle John on the isle of Patmos. Beaten down by the modern world and desperate for answers his years of study have failed to satisfy, Aidan is confronted with astounding insight from the beloved disciple of Jesus. The two begin an extraordinary dialogue of truth and lies, revelation and deception, sorrow and joy. Second Edition.

"*Patmos* is a gateway drug to deep and engaging theology and transformation!"

WM. PAUL YOUNG
#1 *New York Times* best-selling author of *The Shack*

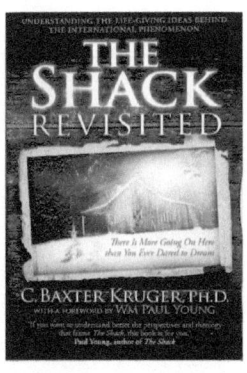

The Shack Revisited

Millions have found their spiritual hunger satisfied by William P. Young's #1 *New York Times* bestseller *The Shack* – the story of a man lifted from the depths of despair through his life altering encounter with God the Father, God the Son and God the Holy Spirit. C. Baxter Kruger's *The Shack Revisited* guides readers Into a deeper understanding of these three persons to help readers have a more profound connection with the core message of *The Shack* – that God is love.

"Baxter Kruger will stun readers with his unique cross of intellectual brilliance and creative genius as he takes them deep into the wonder, worship, and possibility that is the world of *The Shack*."

WM. PAUL YOUNG
Author of *The Shack* and *Eve*

The Parable of the Dancing God

Building on Jesus' story of a father and his two sons, Dr. Kruger's first—and now internationally best-selling—book is a short and powerful picture of the shocking truth about God. Far from being a bookkeeping legalist, who watches us like a hawk to see if we keep His rules, the Father Jesus reveals is a passionate Father who loves us forever, and desires nothing from us except that we know His acceptance and delight and live in their freedom. Loved around the world and used by pastors, therapists and recovery groups everywhere, this little book brings you face to face with the Father heart of God. It is simple, direct and fearlessly beautiful.

"I had tried for 55 years, 11 months, and 16 days to get it right. I mean, tried really hard. It was after 11 o'clock that night when I decided I had to read this little booklet "Parable of the Dancing God" my son-in-law had sent me. When I got to about the third page, I felt like I had been hit in the face with an iron frying pan. I laid back on the pillow, bewildered, and said, "God, have I been thinking wrong all my life?" The response was a simple and clear, "Yes." And that is just the tip of the iceberg.

JULIAN FAGAN,
Attorney, Amory, Mississippi

The Secret
What You Know But Never Knew

This book is a veritable laser beam cutting through the haze of religious confusion. With the turn of a few pages you will see Jesus Christ, not as a spectator who merely watches you from a distance, but as the secret of your very existence. You will come to see your self and your life as you have never seen them. Simple. Clear. Astonishing. This book should be required reading for every person in the Western World.

For more information
about C. Baxter Kruger
go to perichoresis.org

www.ingramcontent.com/pod-product-compliance
Lightning Source LLC
Chambersburg PA
CBHW020343130626
46549CB00003B/1265